Sew Bunting

Sew
Bunting

Simple and stunning garlands to style your home

Debbie Shore

SEARCH PRESS

First published in Great Britain 2014

Search Press Limited
Wellwood, North Farm Road,
Tunbridge Wells, Kent TN2 3DR

Photographs by Garie Hind

Text copyright © Debbie Shore 2013
Photographs © Garie Hind 2013
Design copyright © Search Press Ltd. 2013

ISBN: 978-1-84448-949-7

Suppliers
For details of suppliers, please visit the
Search Press website: www.searchpress.com.

Printed in China

Contents

Simple Bunting,
page 16

Advent Bunting,
page 20

Appliqué Bunting,
page 22

Beach Bunting,
page 26

Blackboard Bunting,
page 30

Country Bunting,
page 50

Halloween Bunting,
page 54

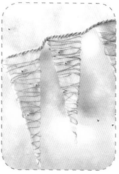

Icicle Bunting,
page 56

Jeans Pocket Bunting,
page 58

Lavender Bunting,
page 60

Santa Bunting,
page 72

Scissor Keeper,
page 76

Scrapbook Bunting,
page 78

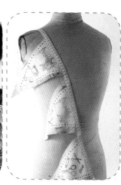

Sewing Room Bunting,
page 80

Steampunk Bunting,
page 82

Introduction 8

Useful tools 10

Basic techniques 12

Useful stitches 14

Projects 16

Index 96

Buttoned Bunting,
page 32

Crazy Patchwork,
page 36

Arty Bunting,
page 40

Lampshade Bunting,
page 44

Heart-felt Bunting,
page 46

Nautical Bunting,
page 62

Oriental Bunting,
page 64

Pelmet Bunting,
page 66

Pocket Bunting,
page 68

Ribbon Bunting,
page 70

Table Bunting,
page 86

Bunting Bag,
page 88

Valentine's Bunting,
page 90

Wedding Bunting,
page 92

Introduction

My name is Debbie Shore. Sewing has always been a part of my life, and when I think about it, to some extent, so has bunting! Royal weddings and jubilees were all the excuse we needed to string rows of patriotic triangles from lamp-post to lamp-post, flying high above trestle tables adorned with brightly coloured cloths and tempting party food.

Bunting has never been more popular that it is now, and there's no reason to take it down after the festivities!

I must admit, when I was asked to write this book, my mouth said 'Yes, I'd love to!' while my head said 'How on earth will I fill all these pages with inspiring ideas on … triangles?', but the more I thought about it, the more my mind raced, and I've come up with some unique designs that I'm sure you'll enjoy making, and that will put personality into a room or brighten up a garden.

I've based each project on one or two metres of bunting but of course you can make it as long or as short as you like, in whatever fabric you wish, and in any colour that takes your fancy. There are no rules, so enjoy!

Acknowledgements

Many thanks to my husband, Garie Hind, who photographed everything so beautifully; models Hettie Baker, Elise Collie and Sadie Collie; and Kimberley Hind, who styled all the photographs in the book.

Useful tools

A basic sewing machine is essential for making bunting – embroidery stitches are fun but you'll only really need a straight stitch. You will also find that a rotary cutter, craft mat and a ruler are extremely useful for accurate and speedy cutting. Specialist rulers are available for cutting fabric into triangles, which you will find invaluable.

Woven cotton works best for bunting as it presses really well and looks crisp. Felt is easy to work with as it doesn't fray and so won't need a lining. I'd steer away from stretch fabrics as they can distort. Calico is a really cheap but quite heavy fabric that can be dyed or painted, so a good choice if you have a lot of bunting to make! Printable cotton used with your computer and printer allows you to make bespoke designs: try scanning in your children's drawings and photographs for unique bunting.

Fusible adhesive web is an adhesive material with a peel-off paper backing. It is a great way of attaching one piece of fabric to another, as in appliqué, without the need for stitching. Simply iron it on to the back of the fabric shape you wish to attach, remove the paper backing and iron the shape on to the background fabric.

You will need two pairs of scissors, one for fabric and one for paper. Pinking shears can be used to give a pretty, decorative edge to felt or to help prevent a fabric from fraying. A repositionable spray glue is useful to hold sections of fabric together before sewing, and a stronger glue, for instance from a glue gun, is perfect for adding buttons or trim. For marking the fabric, use a vanishing fabric marker pen. The ink will gradually disappear, leaving no marks on the fabric.

I use hand-sewing needles for invisible sewing, gathering and closures, and either matching or contrasting threads depending on whether I want the stitching to be visible or not. Don't worry about the type of thread you use – bunting isn't usually put in the wash! You will also need a tape measure, a turning tool to push out the points and corners, and an iron. I use a steam-generator iron as I can leave it on for long periods of time.

Fabric-cutting machines are available from major craft shops as well as on-line suppliers and are well worth investing in if you do a lot of appliqué work or papercrafting. They work with design cards and allow you to cut out complex shapes quickly and easily, including alphabet letters, flowers, animals, snowflakes and other festive and special-celebration icons.

The instructions for the bunting shown here are provided on pages 32–35.

Basic techniques

Cutting the triangles

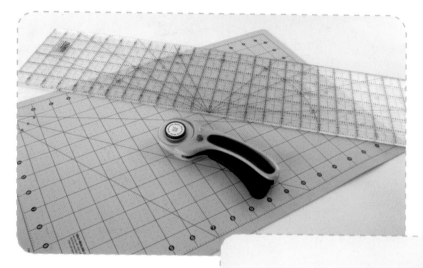

A rotary cutter, craft mat and specialist ruler are indispensable for cutting triangles from fabric.

Cut the length of your triangles in a long strip. Measure and mark the width, and cut, always away from you, with a rotary cutter. Bear in mind that by cutting this way, half of your triangles will be upside down. If your fabric has to be cut in the same direction each time because of the pattern, bear in mind that you'll need twice as much.

Attaching the triangles to the tape

Start in the centre of the ribbon or tape so that you are left with an even tie at each end. I've allowed around half a metre of extra tape at each end of the bunting in this book, but add extra if you need to.

If attaching your pennants to bias-binding tape, fold and press the tape in half lengthwise. Tuck each pennant into the fold and pin it in place. Space them along the tape evenly. Secure by machine stitching along the tape.

Joining bias-binding tape

When making long lengths of bunting, you may need to join two pieces of bias tape together. Place the two pieces face together and at right angles. Then adjust them so you have an overlap of about 0.5cm (¼in). Draw a line diagonally from one right angle to the other, and sew, back-tacking each end. Open up the seam and press.

1

2

3

Useful hints and tips

- Don't use too many embellishments that could make your bunting heavy, as this could distort the shape of the triangles.
- Very fine fabric can become see-through in sunlight.
- If your bunting is for outdoors, be aware of the effects of rain! Cord can stretch when wet, particularly with heavy, wet fabric hanging from it. Colours may run, and certainly keep any fabric you've printed yourself for indoor use only!
- Bunting doesn't have to be made from fabric; plastic, card or wallpaper make for an easy, no-sew banner. Simply staple your decorated pennants on to ribbon for instant impact.

Useful stitches

Machine stitches

Straight stitch
Straight stitch is used to join fabric together, hem or top stitch. Here you see two different lengths of stitch. I use a short stitch to sew the bunting triangles together and a longer stitch for attaching the bias-binding tape or ribbon as it is less likely to pucker.

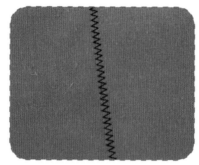

Zig-zag stitch
Zig-zag stitch is used around hems to help stop the fabric fraying. It is also used as a decorative stitch, and can form a dense, solid line. I used this with my Valentine's bunting (see page 90). When choosing a short stitch length, a satin stitch is formed, which is useful for stitching around an appliquéd shape.

Top stitch
Use this on the right side of your fabric as a decorative stitch. Keep it straight, as this stitch line will be seen! To help keep your sewing straight, use the guide on the throat plate of your sewing machine, or mark with tailor's chalk and a ruler and follow this line, rubbing the chalk away afterwards. I've used this stitch on the bias tape at the top of my bunting.

Back stitch
Back stitch is simply straight stitch worked with a long stitch length. It makes a bold, solid line of stitching.

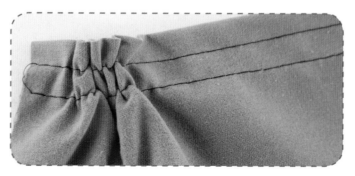

Gathering
Choose a long straight stitch and loosen the tension. Sew along the hem, leaving a long strand of thread at the end. Take the bottom thread and carefully pull the fabric along it. On longer lengths of fabric I recommend you sew a double row of stitches, partly to keep the gathering flat, and partly so you have a back-up if one thread snaps! I used this on the frilled bunting on pages 50–53.

Hand stitches

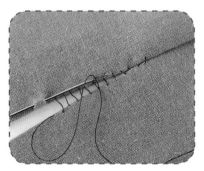

Ladder stitch
This stitch invisibly joins an opening by hand. Try to make the stitches as small as you can.

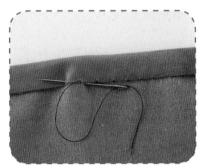

Slip stitch
I use this stitch with bias binding to make a neat finish, though on bunting machine stitch also works well. Keep the stitches small and even for the best finish.

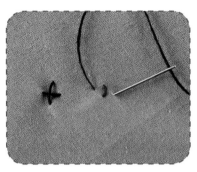

Cross stitch
This simple hand embroidery stitch can be added to your finished bunting to give a pretty home-made feel to your projects.

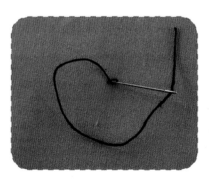

French knots
Another little embroidery stitch made by simply picking up a tiny bit of fabric, wrapping the thread round the needle three or four times, and securing on the back of the fabric.

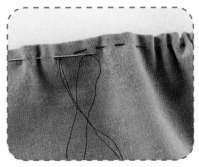

Running stitch
Small running stitches work well as a decorative outline. To form gathers, stitch them across the edge of your fabric or ribbon and gently pull the fabric into gathers.

Back stitch
Back stitch makes a solid line, useful for creating a bold, stitched line when hand stitching.

Simple Bunting

This bunting is lined and stitched into bias-binding tape. It's a simple design but is very neat, showing no raw edges. This style of bunting is used in some of the other projects in this book, so it is a good one to start with. The quantities given are for making two metres (two yards) of bunting, but of course you can make it as long or as short as you like.

What you need

3m (120in) of bias-binding tape, 2.5cm (1in) wide

To make 12 triangles measuring 10cm (4in) across the top and 15cm (6in) deep, you will need a strip of fabric 65 x 15cm (26 x 6in)

Note: if your fabric has a pattern that needs to be a certain way up, you will need to double the length to 130cm (52in)

1 You need to cut twelve triangles from patterned fabric and twelve triangles from plain fabric. Each triangle should measure 10cm (4in) across the top and 15cm (6in) deep.

2 Lay one patterned triangle face up, and place the contrasting triangle face down on top of it.

3 Sew together the two long sides leaving a gap at the top, back-tacking at both the beginning and end.

4 Snip straight across the point, being careful not to cut through the stitches; this lessens the bulk of the fabric so gives a sharper point when turned.

5 Turn the right way out and press.

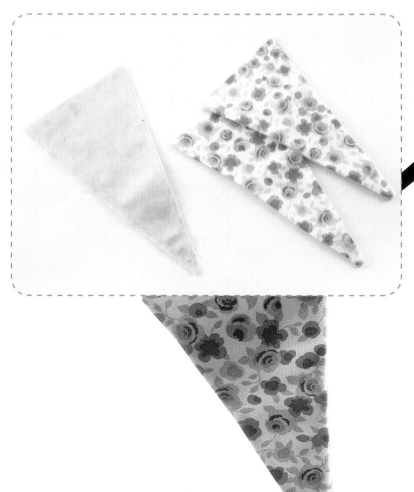

Tip
You may need to trim the top of the triangle with your rotary cutter again to make it neat.

6 Fold your bias tape in half lengthwise and press.

7 Starting at the centre point, slip the triangles inside the bias tape, leaving a gap of 5cm (2in) between each one. Pin them in place as you go.

8 Machine stitch all the way along the bias tape, trapping the pennants as you sew.

Advent Bunting

Pop a little present in each of the twelve pockets for an extra-special treat in the run-up to Christmas! The pockets will take the weight of little gifts like small toys or candy, but be careful of chocolate melting in front of the winter fire! I have used canvas to make the pennants, but any thick cotton or calico will do.

What you need

For 12 pennants you will need:

3.5m (140in) of grey checked ribbon, 1cm (½in) wide

117 x 18cm (46 x 7in) of plain fabric cut into 12 triangles measuring 18cm (7in) across the top and 18cm (7in) in depth

78 x 6.5cm (30 x 2½in) of red gingham cut into 12 squares measuring 6.5 x 6.5cm (2½ x 2½in)

60 x 5cm (24 x 2in) of green gingham cut into 12 squares measuring 5 x 5cm (2 x 2in)

Red embroidery thread

13 buttons

13 strips of contrasting red ribbon 13cm (5in) in length and 1cm (½in) wide

Vanishing fabric marker pen

1 Blanket stitch along two sides of the triangles. This doesn't have to be too neat; the rustic look suits the folksy style of this bunting.

Tip

Many sewing machines have a blanket stitch, so for speed you could use this instead of hand sewing.

2 Take the green gingham squares and draw a number from 1 to 12 on each one using the vanishing fabric marker.

3 Embroider over the numbers using back stitch, then attach each green gingham square to the centre of a red gingham square with a cross stitch in each corner.

4 Place each square in the centre of one of the twelve triangles, and hand sew around three sides to make little pockets. This could also be done on your sewing machine.

5 Arrange the triangles in numerical order, and machine stitch them to the grey ribbon, leaving a gap of around 2.5cm (1in) between each pennant. Fold each piece of red ribbon in half and attach it to the grey ribbon with a button. Embroider a few more cross stitches and stars to your bunting to finish.

Tip

Some simple hand embroidery can add a pretty finishing touch to your bunting.

Appliqué Bunting

This is quick and simple bunting that can be adapted to match your interior décor and personalised with names or pictures. I've cut out my shapes with a fabric-cutting machine, which is well worth the investment if you're cutting a lot of appliqué shapes. If you don't have a cutting machine, use templates to cut out the shapes – either draw these yourself on card or use shop-bought ones. I've also backed my shapes with fusible adhesive web, which cuts down on sewing time!

1 Gather together all the materials you need to make your bunting.

What you need

To make 1m (40in) of bunting:

2m (80in) of green ribbon, 1cm (½in) wide

90 x 30cm (36 x 12in) of patterned fabric cut into 6 squares measuring 15 x 15cm (6 x 6in)

60 x 30cm (24 x 12in) of contrasting fabric cut into 4 squares measuring 15 x 15cm (6 x 6in)

5 appliqué triangles cut from remnants of the patterned and contrasting fabric, measuring 7.5cm (3in) along each side and backed with fusible adhesive web

5 appliqué flowers cut from 51 x 15cm (20 x 6in) white fabric, each measuring approximately 7.5 x 7.5cm (3 x 3in) and backed with fusible adhesive web

12 mini craft pegs

Fabric glue (optional)

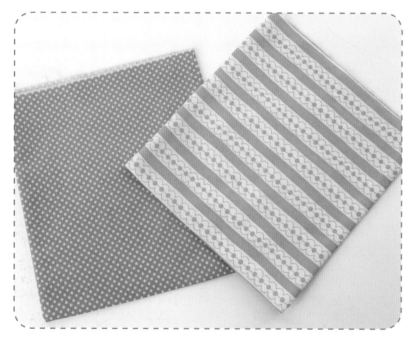

2 Place your squares of fabric together, right sides facing, and sew around three sides.

3 Snip the corners, turn and press.

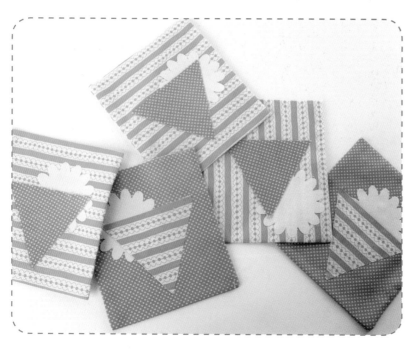

4 Turn in the top of the squares by about 0.5cm (¼in) and press. Do not stitch the seam at this stage.

5 Lay out all five pennants, peel off the paper backing on the appliqué shapes, and arrange the flower and triangle designs on the squares. Vary the positions of the shapes on each pennant. When you're happy with your arrangments, iron the shapes in place.

6 Starting in the centre of the ribbon, pin the pennants along the ribbon, 2.5cm (1in) apart, then top stitch along the ribbon to hold them in place using a zig-zag stitch.

7 Position the little pegs at the corners of the pennants. If you wish, pop a little fabric glue under the pegs so that they don't slip.

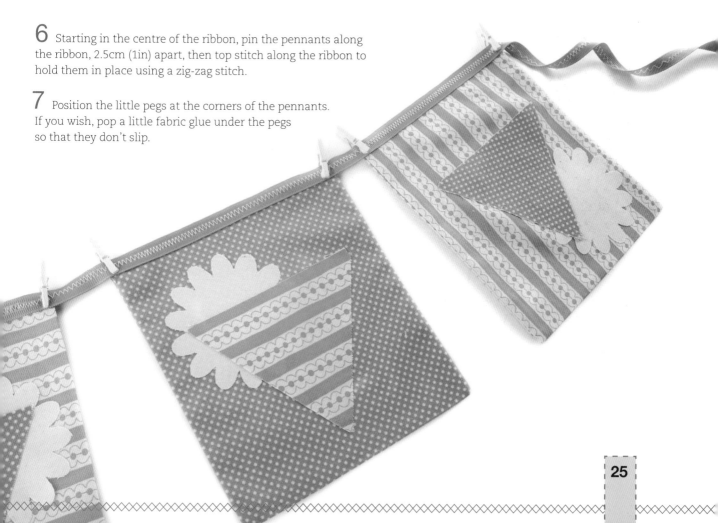

Beach Bunting

If you like to be beside the seaside, you'll enjoy making this deckchair-inspired bunting. The stripy fabric I've chosen reminds me of jolly beach huts, sea shells and sunshine!

For the matching deckchair cover, you will need to use a strong, curtain-weight fabric. Simply remove the existing cover and use this as a template for the new one. Roll the ends of the cover over the bars at the top and bottom of the deckchair seat and staple it in place to secure.

1 Pair up the rectangles of fabric and place them together with right sides facing. Sew around three sides, leaving the top open. Snip the bottom two corners.

2 Turn each pennant right side out and press.

Tip

This bunting works just as well with traditional triangular pennants – follow the simple bunting instructions on pages 16–19.

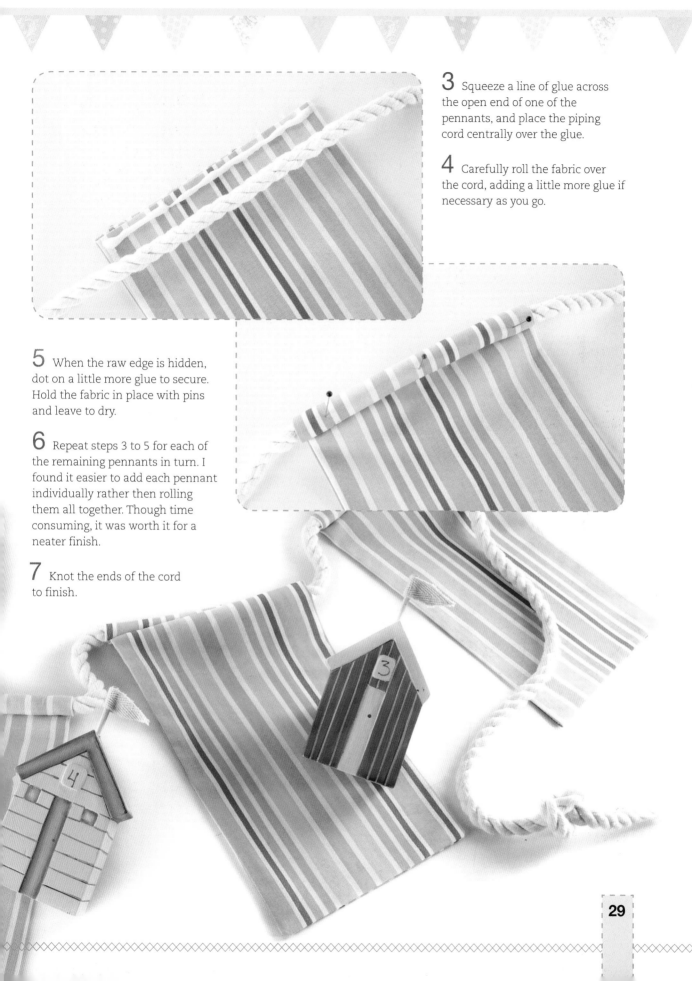

3 Squeeze a line of glue across the open end of one of the pennants, and place the piping cord centrally over the glue.

4 Carefully roll the fabric over the cord, adding a little more glue if necessary as you go.

5 When the raw edge is hidden, dot on a little more glue to secure. Hold the fabric in place with pins and leave to dry.

6 Repeat steps 3 to 5 for each of the remaining pennants in turn. I found it easier to add each pennant individually rather then rolling them all together. Though time consuming, it was worth it for a neater finish.

7 Knot the ends of the cord to finish.

Blackboard Bunting

It's back to school with this nostalgic blackboard bunting! Get your children to draw and write on the triangles, then simply wipe them clean and start again! The blackboard paint stops the fabric from fraying so no hemming is required.

By using paperclips, you can add or take away triangles when adding new pictures or messages. If you want your bunting be more permanent, use brads or paper fasteners to attach the triangles to the tape.

If you need more space, for example to write poetry, use rectangles instead of triangles, and if you want to save your children's masterpieces, spray over the top with varnish.

Tip

To give your bunting a more feminine look, trim your triangles with vintage lace.

Tip

My ribbon already had a line of contrasting stitching down the centre, but you could use plain and add the stitching yourself before attaching the pennants.

1 Place your triangles on the sheet of plastic, and brush with the blackboard paint. This is where the plastic is important; if you use paper, the wet fabric will stick!

What you need

To make 1m (40in) of bunting:

39 x 18cm (15 x 7in) of calico cut into 5 triangles measuring 13cm (5in) across the top and 18cm (7in) in depth

1.5m (60in) of black ribbon, 1cm (½in) wide

1 small pot of blackboard paint and a small paintbrush

Large sheet of plastic

10 paperclips

Chalk

Piece of string about 60cm (24in) long

2 When completely dry, lay the triangles on top of the ribbon, leaving a gap between each one of about 2.5cm (1in). Paperclip them in place.

3 Take the chalk and draw!

4 Tie the chalk to the string, then tie this to the tape so the chalk is always there if you want to add another message or drawing.

Buttoned Bunting

This elegant bunting is pretty enough for the bedroom as well as adding a touch of style to your dining room or living room. Try brass buttons on red fabric for a military feel that's perfect for a boy's bedroom. Or how about tassels instead of buttons – or even both – for a hint of decadence?

I've chosen two different-sized buttons for each pennant and sewn them together for a quirky finishing touch.

What you need

To make 2m (80in) of bunting:

9 squares of patterned fabric in various designs measuring 15 x 15cm (6 x 6in)

9 squares of contrasting fabric for the backing measuring 15 x 15cm (6 x 6in)

14 buttons in various sizes and colours

3m (120in) of blue ribbon, 1cm (½in) wide

1 Take each patterned square and pair it up with a contrasting backing square.

2 Lay the backing fabric on top of the patterned fabric, right sides together. Turn the square diagonally towards you, and make a mark on two sides 10cm (4in) from the point at the top. Join these two marks to the point at the bottom to make a kite shape.

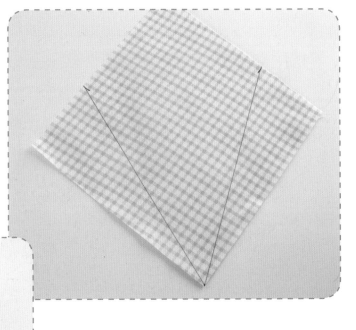

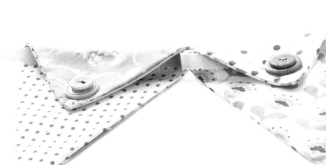

3 Cut along these lines and sew around all four sides.

4 Turn the pennant over and, on the patterned side, draw straight across the kite shape joining the side points together. With scissors, cut across through the top layer of fabric.

5 Snip across the points, turn, then press. Close the opening with a few hand stitches, though this isn't absolutely necessary, then fold over the short point and stitch on a couple of buttons, one on top of the other, to secure.

6 Thread the pennants on to the ribbon. Put a few hand stitches across the back to keep the triangles in place.

Crazy Patchwork

This is a good way of using up scraps of fabric to create a bright, fun decoration.

What you need

To make 2m (80in) of bunting:

72 strips of fabric measuring 15 x 5cm (6 x 2in)

100 x 20.5cm (40 x 8in) of contrasting fabric for the backing cut into 12 triangles measuring 15cm (6in) across the top and 20.5cm (8in) in depth

3m (120in) of bias-binding tape, 2.5cm (1in) wide

1 Place two strips of fabric right sides together, then twist them slightly and sew them together along one edge.

2 Fold back the fabric and press open.

3 Place the next piece of fabric face down on one of the joined strips and twist it in the opposite direction. Sew along the edge as before. Your fabric strips should be taking on a zig-zag look.

4 Fold back the fabric and press open as before.

5 Join five strips together in this way until you have a rectangle measuring approximately 15 x 20.5cm (6 x 8in).

6 Mark the centre point on one of the 15cm (6in) sides and cut from here to the two corners of the facing side to make a triangle.

7 Make eleven more triangles in the same way – twelve all together.

8 Take each patchwork triangle and place it on top of a piece of backing fabric, right sides together. Sew along the two long sides. Snip across the corners.

9 Turn right side out and press. Trim away any untidy edges across the top.

10 Attach the bias-binding tape as in the instructions for simple bunting on pages 18–19.

Tip
If you have embroidery stitches on your sewing machine, you could add a few pretty stitches to the seams before cutting out the triangles.

Arty Bunting

What a lovely way to save and display your little one's artistry! Children will have great fun painting the fabric, and this bunting will add a splash of colour to their bedroom or playroom.

What you need

To make 1m (40in) of bunting:

5 pieces of calico or heavy white cotton fabric measuring 21 x 15cm (8¼ x 6in)

2m (80in) of ribbon, 1cm (½in) wide

Fabric paints in as many colours as you like

Paintbrushes

Jar of water

Sheet of plastic to keep the table top clean

Rotary cutter, clear ruler and cutting mat

1 Cover your table top with plastic, give each of your little ones a piece of fabric and let them paint away! Try not to let the fabric get too wet as it will take a long time to dry.

Tip

I chose plastic as opposed to newspaper to protect the table so that the print wouldn't come off on the fabric.

2 When the masterpieces are finished, leave them to dry completely.

3 Lay the paintings one by one on the cutting mat and cut the fabric into triangle shapes. Do this by placing a ruler over the painting and cutting along the edge using the rotary cutter. Try to keep as much of the artwork in the shape as possible. It doesn't matter if the triangles vary a little – this adds to their charm.

4 Starting at the centre of the ribbon, arrange the triangles evenly behind the ribbon, pin them in place, then sew them on to the ribbon with a straight stitch to secure.

Lampshade Bunting

Take a plain lampshade and bring it right up to date with this pretty mini-bunting trim.

What you need

Plain lampshade: mine measured 96.5cm (38in) in circumference around the base

High tack double-sided tape, 0.5cm (¼in) wide

1m (40in) of ribbon, 1cm (½in) wide

101 x 9cm (40 x 3½in) of fabric cut into 30 triangles measuring 6.5cm (2½in) across the top and 9cm (3½in) in depth

Tip

How about a little glass drop bead on each point to catch the light?

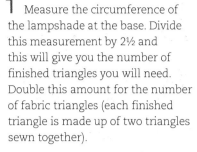

1 Measure the circumference of the lampshade at the base. Divide this measurement by 2½ and this will give you the number of finished triangles you will need. Double this amount for the number of fabric triangles (each finished triangle is made up of two triangles sewn together).

2 Sew pairs of triangles together, right sides facing, leaving the top open for turning. Snip across the corner.

3 Turn the triangles right side out and press.

4 Re-trim across the open top seam to neaten any raw edges.

5 Apply the double-sided tape around the edge of the lampshade, keeping the tape as close to the edge as you can so it cannot be seen when the light shines through.

6 Attach the triangles to the tape, spacing them out evenly. Peel away the backing from the tape as you go.

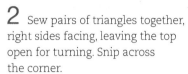

Tip
The triangles can be taken off and re-applied before the ribbon goes on.

7 Add another strip of high tack double-sided tape over the top of the triangles, peel off the backing and attach your ribbon.

Heart-felt Bunting

Felt is such an easy material to work with. It doesn't fray and is available in a wide range of colours. I've chosen vintage shades for my bunting but brights or pastels would work just as well.

When ironing felt, try to use the steam only and avoid touching the fabric with the iron – sometimes it can leave marks as it flattens the plush.

Felt is quite a sturdy fabric so it can be embellished with buttons or ribbons, and don't forget the pinking shears – felt was made for them!

What you need

To make 2m (80in) of bunting:

3m (120in) of bias-binding tape, 2.5cm (1in) wide – mine has a lace edge, but plain bias binding works just as well

8 different-coloured felt squares measuring 20.5 x 20.5cm (8 x 8in) cut into 8 triangles measuring 20.5cm (8in) across the top and 20.5cm (8in) in depth

8 felt triangles of the same size in darker versions of the same colours

A heart-shaped cardboard template measuring around 7.5cm (3in) across and 10cm (4in) down, cut using the template on the facing page

Strong fabric glue

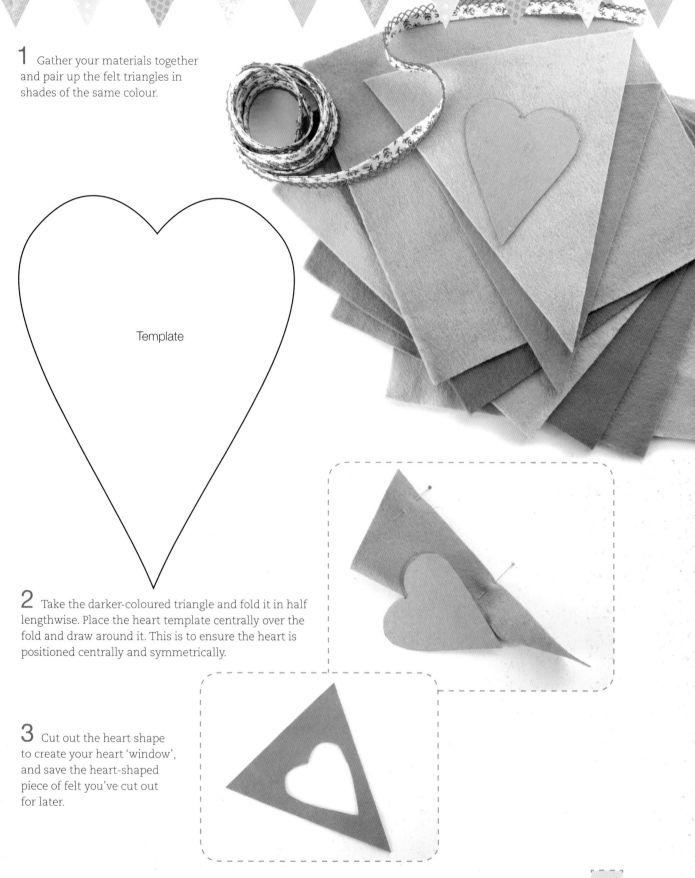

1 Gather your materials together and pair up the felt triangles in shades of the same colour.

Template

2 Take the darker-coloured triangle and fold it in half lengthwise. Place the heart template centrally over the fold and draw around it. This is to ensure the heart is positioned centrally and symmetrically.

3 Cut out the heart shape to create your heart 'window', and save the heart-shaped piece of felt you've cut out for later.

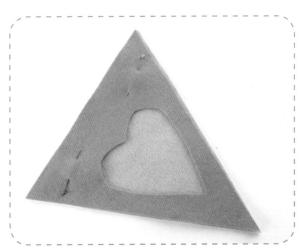

4 Place the dark-coloured triangle over it's lighter partner and pin it in place.

5 If you have embroidery stitches on your sewing machine, now is the time to use them, but a zig-zag or straight stitch would work well too. Sew around the heart, then again along the two long sides of the triangle.

6 Complete all the triangles in this way.

7 Turn the triangles over and simply glue the felt heart cut-outs to the back. I found it neater to glue rather than sew them on, as it was difficult to line up the stitches perfectly.

8 Starting in the centre, stitch the heart pennants to the bias-binding tape leaving 2.5cm (1in) gaps between each one.

Tip

Your 'window' doesn't have to be a heart shape; it could, for instance, be a triangle, flower or circle.

Country Bunting

This bunting is so pretty and feminine, it reminds me of a 1950s-style apron so I put it in the kitchen, although it would work just as well in a girl's bedroom!

What you need

To make 1m (40in) of bunting:

2m (80in) of bias-binding tape, 2.5cm (1in) wide

10 triangles in a variety of different fabrics measuring 15cm (6in) across the top and 15cm (6in) in depth

For the frill, 6m (240in) of fabric, 5cm (2in) wide, folded in half lengthwise and pressed. You could use 2.5cm (1in) wide ribbon instead if you wish

1 Sew the raw edges of the long strip of fabric together with a long straight stitch on your sewing machine, as close as you can to the edge. You could do this by hand if you prefer.

2 Take the bottom bobbin thread and start to pull gently until the whole strip is gathered.

3 Two rows of stitching will help the fabric to lay flat, and don't worry if your thread breaks when pulling as you can always re-sew.

4 Pin the frill to the right side of a triangle, raw edges together. Secure with a hand stitch and remove the pins.

5 Place a second triangle face down over the top, right sides facing, and pin it in place. Hand sew again if you wish, and make sure that the frilled fabric is neatly tucked in at the point of the triangle.

6 Machine stitch along the two frilled sides.

7 Turn in the right way and repeat with the rest of the triangles.

8 Attach the bias binding as explained on pages 18–19.

Attach the bias binding as explained on pages 18–19.

Tip
Try using lace as the frill instead of fabric.

Halloween Bunting

This spooky spider bunting will help keep the ghouls at bay on All Hallow's Eve!

What you need

To make 2m (80in) of bunting:

72 x 18cm (28 x 7in) of orange felt cut into 10 triangles measuring 13cm (5in) across the top and 18cm (7in) in depth

3m (120in) of black ribbon, 0.5cm (¼in) wide

Dark-coloured metallic embroidery thread and embroidery needle

Pencil and ruler

Black ink pad suitable for fabric

Plastic spiders to decorate

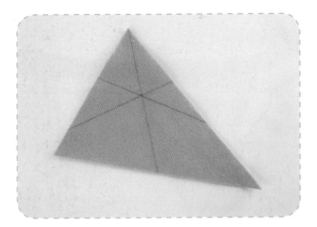

1 Draw three lines across one of the felt triangles, meeting at the centre to make a 'star' shape. Repeat on the remaining triangles, positioning the lines slightly differently on each one.

2 Stitch over these lines in black on your sewing machine. I used a stretch stitch as it's bolder than a straight stitch and breaks less easily when the fabric is stretched. If your machine doesn't have this stitch, a long straight stitch works just as well, or alternatively use a hand-sewn back stitch.

3 Thread your embroidery needle with the metallic thread and, starting near the centre, bring the needle up from the back through one of the stitched lines. Take your needle across to the next line and catch it underneath the stitching. Continue in a spiral until you come to the edge of the triangle.

4 Knot your thread at the back and trim. Repeat on each of the felt triangles. Try to vary the pattern on each one for a more interesting effect.

5 Lay the ribbon over the top of the triangles (it looks quite quirky if they aren't straight) and zig-zag stitch over the top to secure.

6 Take your ink pad and distress the edges of your bunting to give it a dusty look.

7 Hand sew your spiders on to their webs.

Icicle Bunting

Add a twinkle to your tree and a sparkle to the festivities with this frosty icicle bunting. Try other colour combinations to match your Christmas theme – white felt wrapped with pale blue or purple wire, for example, or pink felt wrapped with silver for a romantic look.

What you need

To make 1m (40in) of bunting:

2m (80in) of silver cord, 0.5cm (¼in) wide

23 x 18cm (9 x 7in) of white felt cut into 8 triangles measuring 5cm (2in) across the top and 18cm (7in) in depth

One cardboard triangular template measuring 5cm (2in) across the top and 18cm (7in) in depth

Silver glitter spray

Silver florist's wire

Small silver-coloured beads

Wire cutters

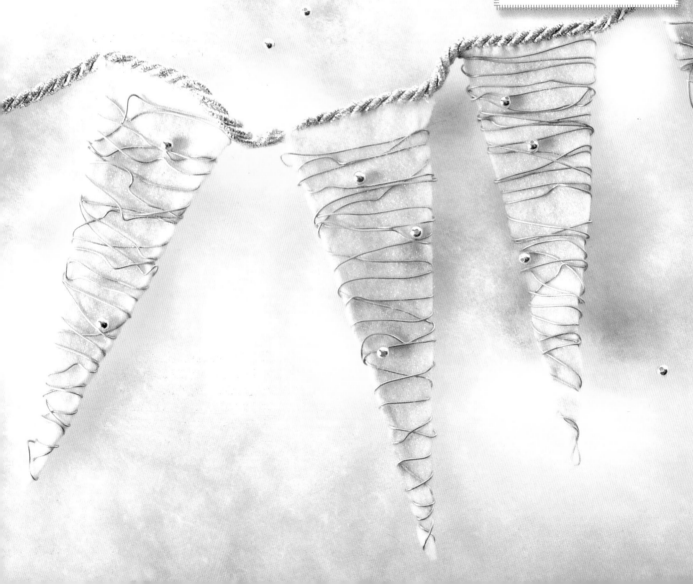

1 Spray one side of the felt triangles with silver glitter spray and leave to dry.

2 Place one triangle glitter-side up on top of the card template and, starting at the top, start to wind the florist's wire around the triangle. It looks better if the wire isn't too neat! Go all the way to the point, then all the way back up. Don't wrap the wire too tightly as it will be difficult to remove the template when you've finished.

3 Cut off the remaining wire with cutters and tuck the end of the wire underneath to avoid a sharp point.

4 Holding the icicle in the palm of one hand, gently pull the template away. Repeat steps 2 to 4 for the remaining triangles.

5 When all eight triangles are finished, hand sew them with an overhand stitch on to the silver cord, starting in the middle and spacing them about 5cm (2in) apart.

6 Glue the silver beads on to the felt as a finishing touch. Alternatively, try threading the beads on to the wire as you wrap. This is more time consuming but creates a lovely effect.

Jeans Pocket Bunting

Never ever throw away old jeans! Practically every part can be re-used, and denim is a lovely fabric to work with, especially when it has developed character with age.

This bunting works well in a child's bedroom. Pens, pencils, hair accessories and jewellery can be stored in the pockets, and the left-over fabric can be used to cover the bed headboard, chairs or cushions.

What you need

To make 2m (80in) of bunting:

Approximately 10 denim pockets, depending on size

3m (120in) of string or rope

Beads, buttons, metal rings, etc. to decorate

Strong fabric glue

Tip

To cut the pockets off the back of the jeans, slip the blade of your scissors just under the edge of the pocket but don't cut through the stitches. Cut through the fabric around the three stitched sides of the pocket. At the top, leave about 2.5cm (1in) of extra fabric as this is where you'll attach the string later.

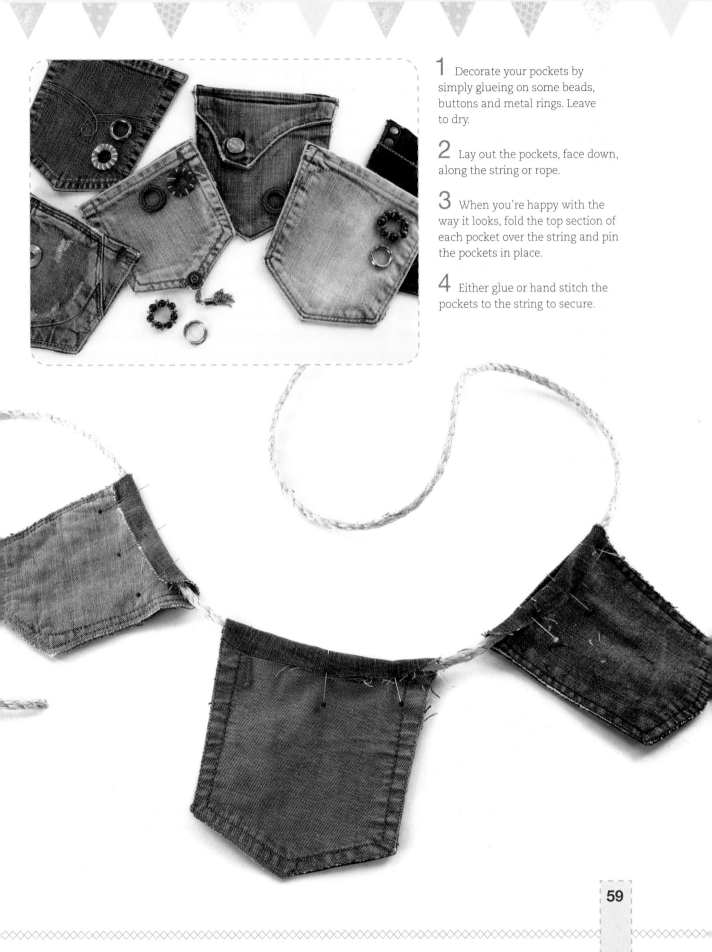

1 Decorate your pockets by simply glueing on some beads, buttons and metal rings. Leave to dry.

2 Lay out the pockets, face down, along the string or rope.

3 When you're happy with the way it looks, fold the top section of each pocket over the string and pin the pockets in place.

4 Either glue or hand stitch the pockets to the string to secure.

Lavender Bunting

Lavender is believed to create a relaxing, restful atmosphere, so this pretty bunting is ideal for the bedroom. String it across a bed headboard or baby cot for a calming effect. I've made the pennants quite small so that they don't overpower the room.

What you need

To make 1m (40in) of bunting:

95 x 13cm (38 x 5in) of fabric cut into 18 triangles measuring 10cm (4in) across the top and 13cm (5in) in depth

1.5m (60in) of coordinating ribbon, 0.5cm (¼in) wide

Large embroidery needle

1m (40in) of ribbon, 0.5cm (¼in) wide, to make bows

1 sachet of dried lavender

Wadding

Tip

If you prefer, you could use pot-pourri or any other scented dried flowers, or leave the pennants unscented if you wish. If the scent fades over time, try adding a spot of essential oil, but be aware that it may stain your fabric.

1 Place pairs of triangles right sides together and sew along the long sides, leaving the tops open.

2 Snip across the point of each pennant, turn and press.

3 Stuff a little wadding into the point of each triangle, followed by a sprinkle of lavender, then fill to the top with wadding. Don't use too much lavender – you'll be surprised how strong it can be.

4 Fold over the raw edges at the top by about 0.5cm (¼in), then hand sew with ladder stitch to close. You'll find that a curve starts to form across the top due to the wadding.

5 Take the embroidery needle and thread it with ribbon. Push the needle through the top corners of the triangles to string them together and arrange them so the spaces in between are even.

6 To stop the pennants moving, attach a small bow to each top corner. Alternatively you could tie little knots in the ribbon between each triangle.

Nautical Bunting

Bunting derived originally from Naval flags, and this striking red, white and blue striped bunting has a strong nautical feel. I tried and failed to find red or blue rings to attach the bunting to the cord, so decided to cover ordinary gold curtain rings and make my own.

What you need

To make 2m (80in) of bunting:

152 x 30.5cm (60 x 12in) of fabric cut into:

12 rectangles measuring 15cm (6in) long and 13cm (5in) wide, and

12 triangles measuring 10cm (4in) across the top and 15cm (6in) in depth

24 curtain rings, 2.5cm (1in) in diameter

Red and blue yarn, about 1m (40in) of each

3m (120in) of cord

All-purpose clear glue

1 Lay the squares in pairs, wrong sides facing. Top stitch all the way around, quite close to the edge, leaving the edges raw.

2 Do the same with the triangles. You should now have six of each.

3 Take your curtain rings and yarn, and dab a tiny dot of glue on the ring. Holding the end of the yarn firmly on the glue, start to wind it around the ring until the ring is completely covered. Cut the yarn and apply another spot of glue to secure. Leave for a few minutes to dry.

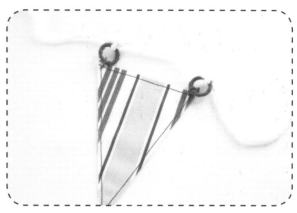

4 Hand sew a covered curtain ring to each of the top corners of the rectangles and triangles.

5 Thread the cord alternately through the triangles and rectangles. Knot each ring in place as you go. Leave about 60cm (24in) of cord free at each end for hanging.

Tip
Try different colour and pattern combinations to suit the style of your room.

Oriental Bunting

What better way to decorate your home for the Chinese New Year celebrations! Bright and bold with a touch of gold: traditional colours to add a pinch of oriental spice!

What you need

To make 2m (80in) of bunting:

82.5 x 20.5cm (33 x 8in) of satin fabric cut into 10 triangles measuring 15cm (6in) across the top and 20.5cm (8in) in depth

5 tassels

3m (120in) of cord

5 buttons

1 Lay the triangles right sides together in pairs and sew them together using your sewing machine along the two long sides. Trim across the point.

Tip

Satin frays easily and can be quite difficult to work with, so try red cotton and hand paint oriental symbols in gold or silver fabric paint instead.

2 Turn each pennant right side out. Fold in the top seams, pin then top stitch them together.

3 Fold the point of each triangle up by about 6.5cm (2½in), threading it through the loop on a tassel. Secure with a button, hand sewn through all the layers of fabric.

4 Lay the cord across the top of the triangles, starting in the centre of the cord, and hand sew it in place with the triangles approximately 4cm (1½in) apart.

Pelmet Bunting

Using fabric to match your décor, this bunting gives a finishing touch to a window, particularly if your window is in a recess and there's no room for curtains.

What you need

To make 1m (40in) of bunting:

162 x 20.5cm (63 x 8in) of patterned fabric cut into 9 rectangles measuring 18cm (7in) by 20.5cm (8in)

162 x 20.5cm (63 x 8in) of plain lining fabric cut into 9 rectangles measuring 18cm (7in) by 20.5cm (8in)

2m (80in) of bias-binding tape, 2.5cm (1in) wide

9 buttons

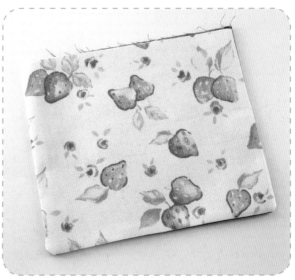

1 Lay one patterned rectangle on top of a plain rectangle, right sides together, and straight stitch around the two shorter sides and one longer side, leaving a gap across the remaining long side. Snip across the two sewn corners.

2 Turn right side out and press.

3 With the lining side facing upwards, take the two bottom corners and fold them to meet in the centre. Pin to secure.

4 Attach a button to the point where the folded corners meet. Hand sew the button straight through to the back of the pennant so that the fold doesn't 'bag'.

5 Repeat for all nine pennants.

6 Attach the pennants to the bias-binding tape, as described on pages 18–19, but leaving no gap in between each one.

Tip
Try attaching a bead, a tassel or a toggle instead of a button.

Pocket Bunting

This really is using all available space for storage! I've kept the triangles quite long so that the contents don't fall forwards and drop out – perfect for pencils, bobbins, ribbons and other lightweight items. If necessary, weigh down the pennants to help them keep their shape by placing a small pebble or curtain weight into each one.

What you need

To make 1m (40in) of bunting:

98 x 25.5cm (39 x 10in) of curtain-weight woven fabric cut into 12 triangles measuring 15cm (6in) across the top and 25.5cm (10in) in depth

39 x 15cm (15 x 6½in) of curtain-weight woven fabric cut into 6 triangles measuring 11cm (4¼in) across the top and 16.5cm (6½in) in depth

1.5m (60in) of bias-binding tape, 2.5cm (1in) wide

1 Fold over the tops of the six smaller triangles by about 0.5cm (¼in) on to the wrong side of the fabric and top stitch to hem.

2 Lay each one on top of a larger triangle, points meeting and with the printed sides of the fabric facing upwards, then lay another large triangle, face down, on top. Pin then stitch very close to the edge along the two long sides to secure. Snip across the point at the bottom, turn and press.

3 Attach the bias-binding tape as described on pages 18–19, leaving no gaps in between the pennants.

Tip

Instead of hemming the smaller triangles, try adding bias-binding tape across the top.

Ribbon Bunting

I created this bunting by accident. I intended to lay ribbon strips across triangles of calico and trim the edges, but as I started to position the ribbons over the calico I rather liked the effect without neatening the edges! It gives a rustic, hand-made feel to the bunting, particularly when using natural-coloured ribbons.

Try using strips of lace for a romantic, 'shabby chic' look, or use strips of fabric with frayed edges for a more relaxed country style.

What you need

To make 1m (40in) of bunting:

2m (80in) of checked ribbon, 1cm (½in) wide

23 x 15cm (9 x 6in) of calico cut into 5 triangles measuring 7.5cm (3in) across the top and 15cm (6in) in depth

Approximately 1.75m (70in) of contrasting ribbon in each of 4 designs (7m or 280in in total)

6 buttons

Strong fabric glue

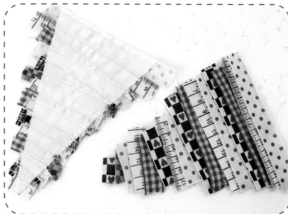

1 Starting at the point of one of the triangles, sew a small piece of ribbon, about 2.5cm (1in) long, across the point. Only stitch along the top edge of the ribbon.

2 Place a second, slightly longer piece of contrasting ribbon at a slight angle on top, so that it just overlaps the stitch line on the previous piece. Sew along the top edge of this piece of ribbon.

3 Carry on sewing in this way, overlapping each piece of ribbon with the one before and angling them all slightly differently, until the whole triangle is covered.

4 Create five pennants in this way and attach them to the checked ribbon with a straight stitch.

5 Fold a piece of checked ribbon, about 7.5cm (3in) in length, in half and sew it by hand in between two pennants. Repeat all the way along the bunting, then either glue or sew a button over the top of each one.

Santa Bunting

This fun Santa Claus bunting will bring joy to the
Christmas festivities for years to come! As I've used felt for
this project, I didn't need to sew at all, but you could use
a decorative stitch around the hat and beard if you prefer.

What you need

To make 1m (40in) of bunting:

2m (80in) of white
piping cord

5 rectangles of red felt each
measuring 25.5 x 10cm
(10 x 4in)

Piece of white felt or
wadding measuring
51 x 63.5cm (20 x 25in)

10 googly eyes

5 red and 5 white pom-poms

Ruler and pencil

Strong fabric glue

1 Take each red felt rectangle and position it with the short sides at the top and bottom. Draw a line across 7.5cm (3in) down from the top.

2 With a ruler, join the centre point of the bottom of the rectangle with each end of the line to form a triangle.

3 In the top section, draw a line from the left end of the line to the top right corner.

4 Repeat this on each red rectangle, varying the shape of the smaller triangle on each one. Cut around the outline to make Santa's chin and hat.

5 For the beard, cut a triangle of white felt or wadding 7.5cm (3in) across the base and 13cm (5in) long for each Santa. Glue this over the chin section of the red felt. Allow to dry.

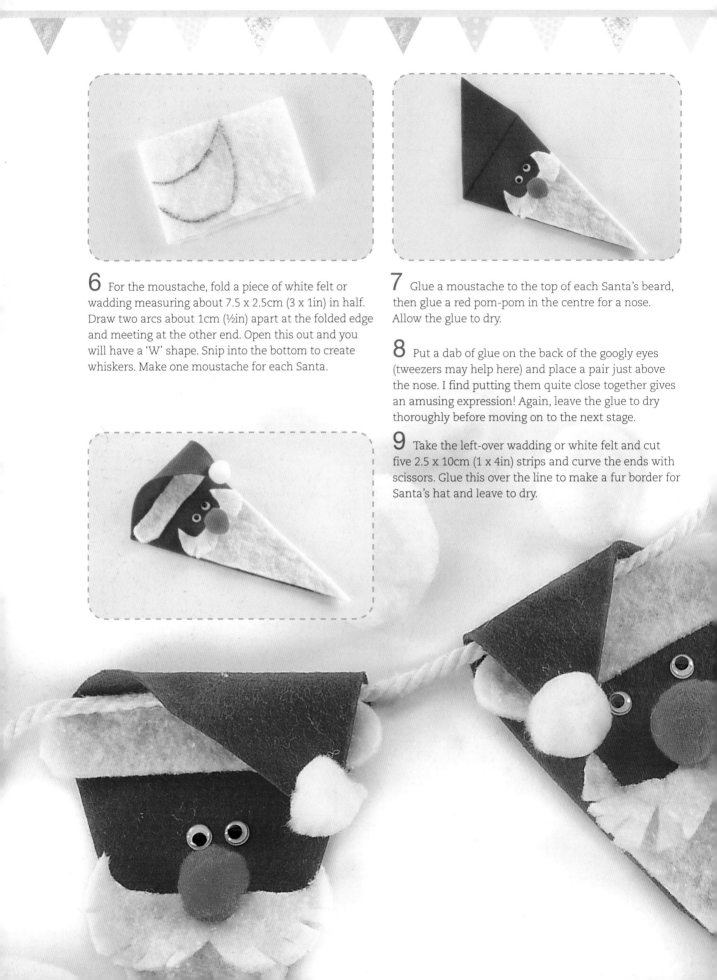

6 For the moustache, fold a piece of white felt or wadding measuring about 7.5 x 2.5cm (3 x 1in) in half. Draw two arcs about 1cm (½in) apart at the folded edge and meeting at the other end. Open this out and you will have a 'W' shape. Snip into the bottom to create whiskers. Make one moustache for each Santa.

7 Glue a moustache to the top of each Santa's beard, then glue a red pom-pom in the centre for a nose. Allow the glue to dry.

8 Put a dab of glue on the back of the googly eyes (tweezers may help here) and place a pair just above the nose. I find putting them quite close together gives an amusing expression! Again, leave the glue to dry thoroughly before moving on to the next stage.

9 Take the left-over wadding or white felt and cut five 2.5 x 10cm (1 x 4in) strips and curve the ends with scissors. Glue this over the line to make a fur border for Santa's hat and leave to dry.

10 Arrange the Santas evenly along the piping cord, starting in the middle of the cord. When you are happy with their positions, lay a line of glue across the top of the fur trims and lay the piping cord down over the top to secure.

11 When the glue is dry, fold over the top of the hat, glue it in position and attach a white pom-pom.

Tip

Felt lends itself to hand stitching, so why not decorate Santa's hat with a few blanket and cross stitches?

Scissor Keeper

This clever bunting will keep your embroidery scissors, seam rippers and tailor's chalk in a place where you can find them! I've used glass beads as weights so that the pennants don't topple forwards when full. Of course, you can store anything you wish in the pockets – pens, pencils and paintbrushes, perhaps, or make-up brushes, hairbrushes and combs. Alternatively, pop a little pot-pourri or lavender into the sachets to help fragrance your room.

1 Fold each square of fabric in half corner to corner, right sides together, to make eight triangles. Use your sewing machine to sew along the two open sides, leaving a gap of around 4cm (1½in) for turning. Snip across the corners.

2 Turn each triangle right side out and press. There is no need to sew the opening closed.

3 Lay the triangle flat, with the long straight side towards you. Take the left and right points and fold them together and upwards to form a diamond shape. Hand stitch the edges together with ladder stitch.

4 Fold over the top of the diamond shape and put a few stitches at the point to secure.

5 Add your beads to the bottom of the pennants.

6 Thread the ribbon through the tops of the pennants. When you're happy with their positions, dab a little glue on the inside where it won't be seen to secure.

Scrapbook Bunting

An interesting and unusual way to display your favourite photographs, or decorate a party room with pictures of the birthday boy or girl growing up!

What you need

To make 1m (40in) of bunting:

12 digital photos and access to a printer

12 sheets of printable fabric

1½m (60in) of ribbon, 1cm (½in) wide

Strong fabric glue (gel is best for a 3D effect)

Buttons, ribbon tied into bows, lace and any other embellishments you can find

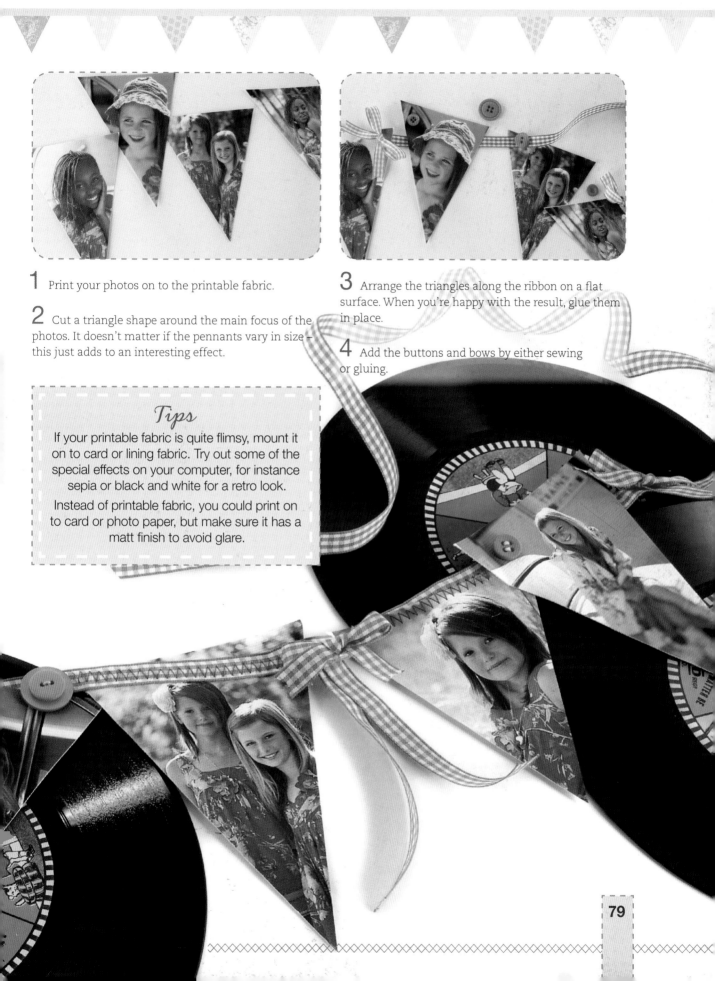

1 Print your photos on to the printable fabric.

2 Cut a triangle shape around the main focus of the photos. It doesn't matter if the pennants vary in size – this just adds to an interesting effect.

3 Arrange the triangles along the ribbon on a flat surface. When you're happy with the result, glue them in place.

4 Add the buttons and bows by either sewing or gluing.

Tips

If your printable fabric is quite flimsy, mount it on to card or lining fabric. Try out some of the special effects on your computer, for instance sepia or black and white for a retro look.

Instead of printable fabric, you could print on to card or photo paper, but make sure it has a matt finish to avoid glare.

Sewing Room Bunting

A fun decoration for your sewing area! I have printed on the sewing-themed designs by hand using rubber stamps, but if you prefer use a cotton fabric pre-printed with a suitable design.

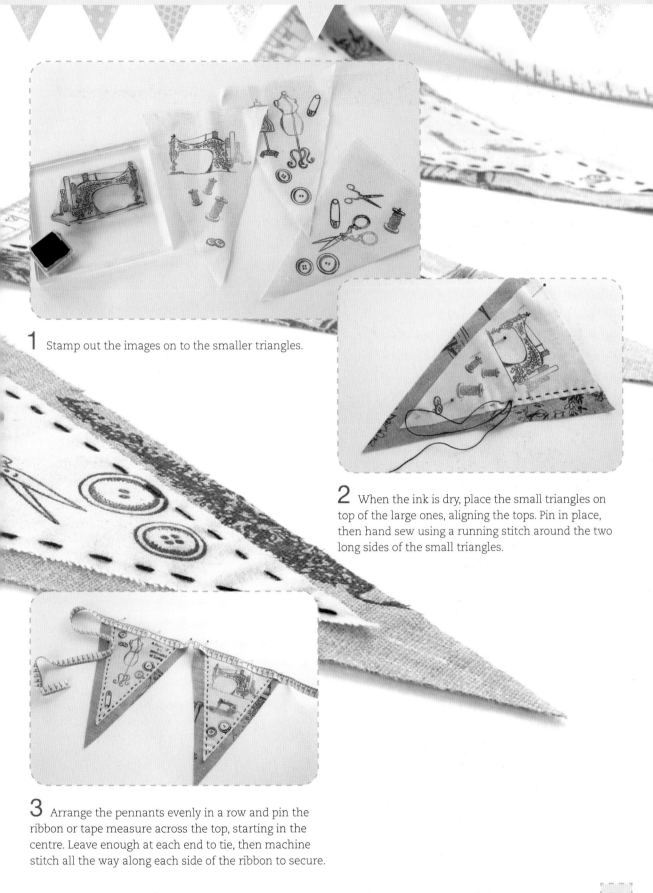

1 Stamp out the images on to the smaller triangles.

2 When the ink is dry, place the small triangles on top of the large ones, aligning the tops. Pin in place, then hand sew using a running stitch around the two long sides of the small triangles.

3 Arrange the pennants evenly in a row and pin the ribbon or tape measure across the top, starting in the centre. Leave enough at each end to tie, then machine stitch all the way along each side of the ribbon to secure.

Steampunk Bunting

Think nineteenth-century science fiction, the steam era, keys, chains and timepieces, and you're thinking steampunk! I spray-painted my hessian with black paint to age it and make it look dusty, while the contrast of the black and white striped background fabric gives a clean edge and makes the detail stand out.

I couldn't find black chain so I spray-painted a length of gold chain, and my watch parts were bought from an auction site at very little cost. The other embellishments were salvaged from old pieces of junk jewellery.

What you need

To make 1m (80in) of bunting:

45 x 18cm (18 x 7in) of hessian cut into 5 triangles measuring 15cm (6in) across the top and 18cm (7in) in depth

1m (80in) of black and white striped cotton fabric

2m (80in) of chain or black ribbon, 1cm (½in) wide

Black spray paint

10 safety pins

A selection of chains, watch parts, cogs and washers to decorate

Strong fabric glue

Cutting mat, rotary cutter and rectangular ruler for cutting 45° angles

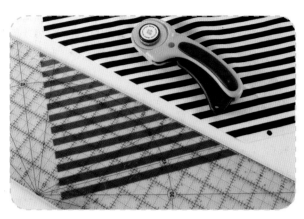

1 Spray-paint your hessian triangles with bursts of paint to give them a dusty, aged look and leave to dry. If possible, spray outside, but if you need to spray indoors, make sure the room is well-ventilated and protect your furnishings and carpets.

2 Take the striped fabric, measure 20.5cm (8in) along each side from one corner, and cut across the corner at a 45° angle.

3 Starting from this cut line as the base, cut a strip of fabric at right angles to it, 10cm (4in) wide.

4 Repeat steps 2 and 3 for the opposite angle. Cut two more 10cm (4in) strips from each corner. The small, cut-off triangles can be discarded.

5 Lay the strips you've cut from each side together, matching the stripes. You'll see the chevrons taking shape.

6 Pin then sew the pairs of strips together with a 0.5cm (¼in) seam allowance, matching up the stripes at the centre seam. Press.

7 Measure and cut your triangles 18cm (7in) across the top and 20.5cm (8in) deep, with the point of each triangle on the centre seam. It doesn't really matter which way up your chevrons are facing.

8 Place the hessian triangles centrally over the chevrons.

9 Using a fine zig-zag stitch, sew the two pieces together.

10 Now for the fun bit! Take your embellishments and arrange them on the pennants. Hand stitch the larger pieces and chains in place, and use fabric glue to secure the smaller pieces. Place heavier decorations towards the bottom of the triangles to help them hang better.

11 Lay out all the pennants evenly in a row and place the safety pins in each top corner, then attach the pennants to either your ribbon or chain.

Table Bunting

This pretty bunting gave back life to an old metal garden table and would work just as well with a wooden table, round or square. My table measures 1.6m (63in) around the outside, for which I needed 12 triangles altogether. For a larger or smaller table, alter the number of triangles accordingly.

What you need

For a 1.6m (63in) circumference table:

84 x 18cm (33 x 7in) of fabric cut into 12 triangles measuring 13cm (5in) across the top and 18cm (7in) in depth

85 x 18cm (33 x 7in) of coordinating lining fabric cut into 12 triangles measuring 13cm (5in) across the top and 18cm (7in) in depth

2m (80in) of matching ribbon, 2.5cm (1in) wide

A piece of fabric 61 x 61cm (24 x 24in) to cover the table top

Wadding of the same size

Super-sticky double-sided tape

Fabric glue

1 Lay the wadding on top of the table and, holding it in place with one hand in the centre, trim it back with scissors until it is the same size as the table top.

2 Attach a strip of double-sided tape around the edge of the table top. Lay your square of fabric face up centrally over the table and smooth it over the edges, adhering it to the double-sided tape. Trim away the excess fabric but leave enough to tuck under the table top to make it neat. Another strip of double-sided tape under the lip of the table will secure it.

3 Make up the bunting by stitching the triangles to the ribbon, leaving only a small gap in between each (see pages 18–19).

4 Stick another strip of double-sided tape around the edge of the table and apply the bunting. Overlap the ends where they meet and secure them with a dab of fabric glue. If you wish, add a little bow to hide the join.

Bunting Bag

Decorate a plain tote bag with a string of mini bunting and bring it right up to date.

What you need

A plain canvas tote bag measuring approximately 40.5 x 40.5cm (16 x 16in)

11 squares of fabric in different designs, each measuring 7.5cm (3in) square

1.5m (59in) of decorative cord trim

Fabric glue

Buttons or felt shapes to decorate

Tip

The little bunting shapes can also be used to trim cushion covers, teacloths or even towels.

1 Take each square of fabric, fold it in half and press.

2 Fold both corners from the folded edge up to the centre of the opposite edge to form a triangle.

3 You should now have 11 triangles. Sew across the top of each to keep the shape, using a straight stitch on your sewing machine.

4 Drape the cord over your tote bag to use as a guide for positioning the triangles. Pin then glue the triangles in place with a dab of fabric glue.

5 Glue the cord in place over the tops of the triangles, dabbing a little glue on the ends of the cord to stop it fraying.

6 Hand sew buttons or felt shapes to the ends of the cord to hide them.

7 Attach a cord around the top of the bag and add some buttons or felt shapes to finish.

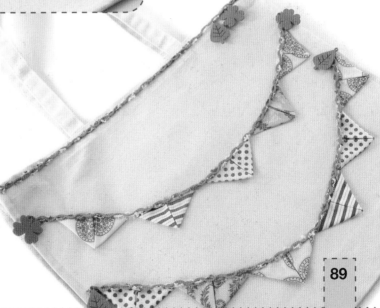

Valentine's Bunting

Add a touch of romance to your Valentine's dinner with this pretty bunting. For a completely different look, try replacing the hearts with felt flowers or butterflies – just right for a summer party!

What you need

To make 1m (40in) of bunting:

45 x 18cm (18 x 7in) of fabric cut into 5 triangles measuring 15cm (6in) across the top and 18cm (7in) in depth

45 x 18cm (18 x 7in) of coordinating fabric cut into 5 triangles the same size as above

2m (80in) of bias-binding tape, 2.5cm (1in) wide

5 felt hearts, about 7.5cm (3in) square. I cut my hearts freehand but you could use a punch, cutting machine or a template downloaded from the internet.

1 Cut each triangle in half lengthwise.

2 Take away one half of each triangle and replace it with one in the contrasting fabric, then sew them back together again. Press the seam, and trim off any excess fabric at the point.

3 Place the triangles face to face to make five pennants and sew them together along the two long sides. Snip the point for turning, turn right side out and press again.

4 Place the felt hearts in the centre of each triangle, pin, then satin stitch down the centre to secure.

5 Attach the pennants to the bias-binding tape following the instructions on pages 18–19.

Wedding Bunting

This elegant bunting is easy to make and looks spectacular! It is only suitable for use indoors as the ink would run if it rained, but drape it around the walls and windows and across the front of the top table for a stunning finishing touch to your special day.

Musical scores are freely available to download from the internet. Alternatively, stamp a design over fabric, as in the sewing room bunting project on pages 80–81, or use a pre-printed fabric in a suitable design.

Tip
Change the colours to match the wedding, and instead of a musical score try printing photographs of the happy couple on to the fabric.

1 Make up a jug of tea with the two teabags. The stronger the tea, the deeper the colour of your stain. Paint the tea over the printable fabric, not too evenly, to create a vintage look.

2 Allow the fabric to dry thoroughly, otherwise your ink will smudge.

What you need

To make 2m (80in) of bunting:

8 sheets of printable white cotton fabric measuring 30 x 21cm (11¾ x 8¼in)

93 x 25.5cm (36 x 10in) of cream lining fabric cut into 8 triangles measuring 20.5cm (8in) across the top and 25.5cm (10in) in depth

Distress ink pad and sponge

2 teabags

Paintbrush

3m (120in) of cream lace, 4cm (1½in) wide

16 hat pins with pearl beads

16–24 miniature craft flowers

Approximately 2m (80in) of assorted lace and ribbon for bows

Access to a computer and a printer

Gold-coloured 2.5cm (1in) curtain rings, decorative bells and beads to embellish

3 Print off your music score on to the ten sheets of stained printable fabric. It could be the Wedding March or any suitable piece of music.

4 Making sure the ink is dry, mark the centre point at the bottom of each sheet. Draw a line from this point to each top corner to make a triangle.

5 Cut out each triangle and apply distress ink around the edges of each one using the sponge.

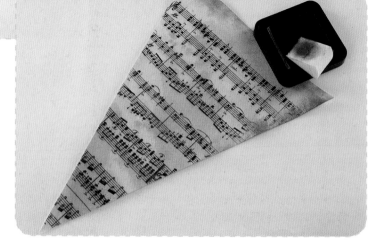

6 When dry, sew the printed triangles to the lining, right sides together, leaving the top open for turning.

7 Snip across the points, turn right side out and press.

8 Fold the top edges of each triangle inwards to make a neat edge and press.

9 Pin each pennant to the long piece of lace, starting in the centre and with a gap of around 5cm (2in) between each one. Machine stitch all the way along the lace with a zig-zag stitch to secure.

10 Make up eight double bows from the lace and ribbon, and push two hat pins and two or three little flowers through the centre knot. Add a dab of fabric glue to secure everything firmly.

11 Lay your bunting flat, one section at a time, and either glue or hand stitch a bow to the top right-hand corner of each triangle.

12 To weight the pennants, hand sew a bead or bell to each point. Add pairs of brass curtain rings and little lace bows here and there to decorate.

Index

adhesive 10, 24, 25, 28, 29, 46, 49, 58, 59, 62, 70, 71, 72, 74, 75, 76, 78, 79, 82, 84, 86, 87, 88, 89
appliqué 10, 14, 22–25

back stitch 14, 15, 21, 54
beads 56, 57, 58, 59, 67, 76, 77, 94, 95
bias-binding tape 12, 13, 14, 15, 16, 18, 19, 36, 39, 46, 49, 50, 53, 66, 67, 68, 90, 91
blanket stitch 21, 75
buttons 10, 20, 21, 32–35, 46, 58, 59, 64, 65, 66, 67, 70, 71, 78, 79, 88, 89

calico 10, 20, 31, 40, 70
canvas 20, 80, 88
Chinese New Year 64
Christmas 20, 56–57, 72–75
cord 13, 28, 29, 56, 57, 62, 63, 64, 65, 72, 75, 88, 89
cotton 10, 20, 40, 64, 82
craft mat 10, 12
cross stitch 15, 21, 75
curtain rings 62, 63, 94, 95
cutting out triangles 12

denim 58–59
distressing 55, 94
drawing 10, 30, 31
dyeing 10

embroidery 10, 15, 21, 39, 48

fabric-cutting machines 10, 22, 90
felt 10, 46–49, 54–55, 56–57, 72, 73, 74, 88, 89, 90, 91
flowers 24, 49, 90, 94
French knots 15
fusible adhesive web 10, 22, 24

gathering 10, 14, 15, 51
gingham 20, 21
glue see adhesive

Halloween 54–55
hand stitching 15, 21, 35, 51, 52, 54, 55, 57, 59, 61, 63, 65, 67, 75, 77, 81, 84, 89, 95
hearts 46–49, 90–91
hessian 82, 83, 84

lace 30, 53, 70, 78, 94, 95
ladder stitch 15, 61, 77
lampshade 44–45
lavender 60–61, 76
lining fabric 10, 16, 66, 67, 79, 86, 94, 95

machine stitching 14, 19, 52, 81, 95
mini bunting 44–45, 88–89

needles 10

painting 10, 40–43, 64, 82, 83
patchwork 36–39
photographs 10, 78, 79, 93
pinking shears 10, 46
pom-poms 72, 74, 75
printable cotton 10, 43, 78, 79, 94

ribbon 12, 13, 14, 20, 21, 24, 25, 30, 31, 34, 35, 40, 42, 44, 45, 46, 50, 54, 55, 60, 61, 70–71, 76, 77, 78, 80, 81, 82, 84, 86, 94
rotary cutter 10, 12, 18, 40, 42, 82
running stitch 15, 81

satin 64
satin stitch 14, 91
scissors 10
sewing machine 10, 14, 21, 39, 48, 51, 54, 64, 77, 89
slip stitch 15
specialist ruler 10, 12, 82
stamping 80, 81, 93
steampunk 82–85
straight stitch 10, 14, 42, 48, 51, 54, 66, 71, 89
stretch stitch 54

table 86–87
tassels 32, 64, 65, 67
templates 22, 27, 46, 56, 57, 90
top stitch 14, 25, 65, 68
trim 10

Valentine's 90–91
vanishing fabric marker pen 10, 20, 21

wadding 60, 61, 72, 73, 74, 86, 87
wedding 92–95

zig-zag stitch 14, 25, 48, 55, 84, 95